Duckling

AT HOME ON THE POND

WRITTEN BY SARAH TOAST
ILLUSTRATED BY JUDITH LOVE

Publications International, Ltd.

It is summer, and Mother Duck is making a nest. In a clump of reeds near the edge of the pond, Mother Duck finds a hollow place in the ground. She lines it with grass and soft cattail stems.

Mother Duck lays her nine smooth eggs. She plucks soft feathers from her breast to line the nest.

Mother Duck sits on her nine eggs for many days and nights. Whenever she leaves the nest, she covers her eggs with a soft blanket of down to hide them and keep them warm.

At last Mother Duck hears the "pip-pip" of her ducklings working to get out of their shells. The last little duckling to break out of its shell is Dabble.

Mother Duck protects her new ducklings by rubbing her tummy feathers over them in the nest. Now the ducklings are waterproof. They will stay warm and dry when they swim.

Mother Duck can waterproof her own feathers by combing oil into them with her bill. The oil that she uses comes from a place near her tail.

While the ducklings are resting in their nest, a skunk comes to the water's edge for a drink. Mother Duck and the ducklings try to stay perfectly still and quiet so the skunk will not notice them.

Mother Duck's spotted brown feathers and the stripes on her ducklings blend in with the tall grasses and reeds.

Dabble is a special type of duck known as a dabbler duck. She sees Mother Duck taking care of her brothers and sisters. She knows that her mother will take good care of her, too.

The tiny ducklings are only a few hours old, but they can run. They follow their mother down to the water's edge for their very first swim.

Dabble is the very first young duckling to jump into the water after Mother Duck. Her sisters and brothers gleefully jump in after her. They bob on the water like balls of fluff.

What a glorious and fun pond! Dabble is dazzled by a dragonfly that lands on a nearby lily pad. She stares at a caterpillar on a cattail leaf.

Now Dabble is getting quite hungry, and she knows exactly what to do. She tips up her tail and stretches her bill down to the muddy bottom of the pond to find plenty of plants, roots, and seeds.

Dabble enjoys dipping down to look for food underwater, then popping up again to see where Mother Duck is.

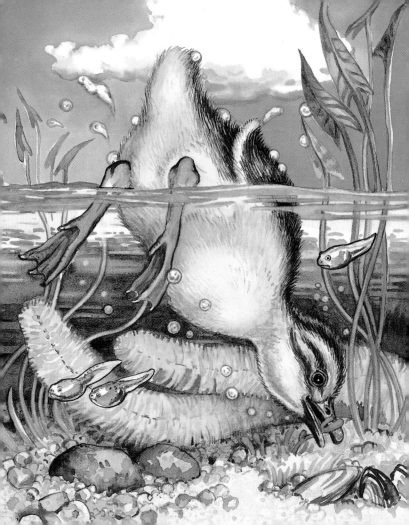

Dabble watches a colorful butterfly flitting among the reeds in the pond. Then Dabble dips down to enjoy another nibble. She lifts her tiny head to quack hello to a red-winged blackbird.

Mother Duck dips down to get something to eat for herself. Underwater, Mother Duck sees a big snapping turtle swimming toward her little ducklings.

Just as quick as a quack, Mother Duck calls out for her ducklings to return to shore, but Dabble is underwater and doesn't hear her.

Mother Duck swims swiftly over to Dabble and gets between Dabble and the snapping turtle. Dabble pops up and swims to shore with Mother Duck, and the turtle swims away.

That night all the ducklings sleep, warm and safe in the nest after their busy first day in the world. Dabble is dreaming of tomorrow, when she will see the bright butterfly again.